C000150598

FOR A

Fantastic

TEACHER

summersdale

FOR A FANTASTIC TEACHER

Summersdale Publishers Ltd
46 West Street
Chichester
West Sussex
PO19 1RP
UK

www.summersdale.com

Printed and bound in China.

ISBN: 978-1-84953-289-1

Substantial discounts on bulk quantities of Summersdale books are available to corporations, professional associations and other organisations. For details contact Summersdale Publishers by telephone: +44 (0) 1243 771107, fax: +44 (0) 1243 786300 or email: nicky@summersdale.com.

To............................

From............................

The mediocre teacher tells. The good teacher explains. The superior teacher demonstrates. The great teacher inspires.

WILLIAM ARTHUR WARD

A teacher affects eternity;
he can never tell where
his influence stops.

HENRY BROOKS ADAMS

When a teacher calls a
boy by his entire name, it
means trouble.

MARK TWAIN

Among fictional schools, Hogwarts was voted the most popular school people wished they could go to, closely followed by St Trinian's.

I believe effective leaders are, first and foremost, good teachers.

JOHN WOODEN

Great teachers...

... provide their students with
all the learning tools they need.

They may forget what you said, but they will never forget how you made them feel.

CARL W. BUECHNER

Education is not the filling of a pail, but the lighting of a fire.

WILLIAM BUTLER YEATS

You deserve
an award for:

Giving the Most
Interesting Lessons.

The highest result of education is tolerance.

HELEN KELLER

I like a teacher who gives you something to take home to think about besides homework.

LILY TOMLIN AS 'EDITH ANN'

In ancient Greece teachers were paid higher wages than skilled craftsmen and received gifts from citizens; the highest paid were music teachers.

A hundred years from now... the world may be different, because I was important in the life of a boy.

FOREST E. WITCRAFT

Great
teachers...

... inspire their students to
think beyond their books.

It is the mark of an educated mind to be able to entertain a thought without accepting it.

ARISTOTLE

Education's purpose is to replace an empty mind with an open one.

MALCOLM FORBES

Somewhere, something incredible is waiting to be known.

CARL SAGAN

You deserve an award for:

The Achievements of your Students, because they're yours too.

I had a terrible education. I attended a school for emotionally disturbed teachers.

WOODY ALLEN

*For every person wishing
to teach, there are thirty
not wanting to be taught.*

SELLAR AND YEATMAN,
AND NOW ALL THIS

The teacher should never lose his temper in the presence of a class. If a man, he may take refuge in profane soliloquies...

WILLIAM LYON PHELPS

Fascinating Fact!

Maya Angelou, Gene Simmons, William Golding, Sting and Stephen King were all teachers before they were famous.

If you think education is expensive, try ignorance.

ANDY MCINTYRE

Great
teachers...

... always give us the
grades we deserve.

Discover wildlife:

be a teacher!

ANONYMOUS

*I've learned that I like
my teacher because
she cries when we
sing 'Silent Night'.*

CHILD, AGE 7

You deserve
an award for:

Being a Teacher
and a Friend.

Just as in real life, my problems may have several answers. This irritates everyone.

OLE HALD,
MATHEMATICS TEACHER

*Nine-tenths of education
is encouragement.*

ANATOLE FRANCE

Over half of people surveyed believed that teachers were the nation's worst dressed profession. And the judges of this? Parents.

The main purpose of education is to keep them off the streets. The teachers, I mean.

ANONYMOUS

Great
teachers...

... are never afraid to take
a hands-on approach.

What sculpture is to a block of marble, education is to a human soul.

JOSEPH ADDISON

It is what we think we know already that often prevents us from learning.

CLAUDE BERNARD

A teacher's purpose is not to create students in his own image, but to develop students who can create their own image.

ANONYMOUS

You deserve an award for:

Telling the
Coolest Stories.

A schoolmaster should have an atmosphere of awe, and walk wonderingly, as if he was amazed at being himself.

WALTER BAGEHOT

Headmasters have powers at their disposal with which Prime Ministers have never yet been invested.

WINSTON CHURCHILL

*Better than a thousand
days of diligent study
is one day with a
great teacher.*

JAPANESE PROVERB

To Be and To Have, Dead Poets' Society and *To Sir with Love* are just a few of the many great films made about teachers.

Sixty years ago I knew everything; now I know nothing; education is a progressive discovery of our own ignorance.

WILL DURANT

Great
teachers...

... stress the importance
of the little details.

Teachers are expected to reach unattainable goals with inadequate tools. The miracle is that at times they accomplish this impossible task.

HAIM G. GINOTT

*What office is there which involves more responsibility...
than teaching?*

HARRIET MARTINEAU

You deserve
an award for:

Cracking the
Funniest Jokes.

Every truth has four corners: as a teacher I give you one corner, and it is for you to find the other three.

CONFUCIUS

Once children learn how to learn, nothing is going to narrow their mind. The essence of teaching is to make learning contagious, to have one idea spark another.

MARVA COLLINS

Giving an apple to your teacher is a tradition in parts of Europe and North America. The term 'apple-polisher' was first used in the 1920s to refer to a creep or toady.

To know how to suggest is the great art of teaching.

HENRI-FRÉDÉRIC AMIEL

Great teachers...

... make learning fun!

*Who dares to teach must
never cease to learn.*

JOHN COTTON DANA

A teacher who is attempting to teach without inspiring the pupil with a desire to learn is hammering on a cold iron.

HORACE MANN

*If there were no schools
to take the children
away from home part
of the time, the insane
asylum would be
filled with mothers.*

EDGAR WATSON HOWE

You deserve
an award for:

Valiant Effort in
putting up with us!

The best teachers teach from the heart, not from the book.

ANONYMOUS

*Ideal teachers are those
who use themselves
as bridges over which
they invite their
students to cross.*

NIKOS KAZANTZAKIS

*I am not a teacher
but an awakener.*

ROBERT FROST

Fascinating Fact!

Years after you leave,
teachers often still
remember you — if
you were very good or
very bad, at least!

I see it as one of my prime duties as a scholar-teacher to stretch students' abilities, open their eyes, and require of them as much as I think they can produce.

MARK GRIFFITH,
CLASSICS TEACHER

Great
teachers...

... know that big things grow
from the seed of knowledge.

*The important thing is not
so much that every child
should be taught,
as that every child should
be given the wish to learn.*

JOHN LUBBOCK

If a seed of a lettuce will not grow, we do not blame the lettuce. Instead, the fault lies with us for not having nourished the seed properly.

BUDDHIST PROVERB

You deserve
an award for:

Taking an Interest
above and beyond
the call of duty.

The teacher who is indeed wise does not bid you to enter the house of his wisdom but rather leads you to the threshold of your mind.

KHALIL GIBRAN

Teachers should be the highest paid employees on earth.

ANONYMOUS

The United Nations' (UN) World Teachers' Day is celebrated on 5 October, recognising the invaluable role of teachers across the globe.

A short philosophy
of teaching might be,
'Love your subject and
convey that love; all
else is secondary.'

J. DAVID JACKSON,
PHYSICS TEACHER

Great
teachers...

. . . remember that sometimes
play is as important as work.

No man can be a good
teacher unless he has
feelings of warm affection
toward his pupils.

BEATRAND RUSSELL

It is the supreme art of the teacher to awaken joy in creative expression and knowledge.

ALBERT EINSTEIN

*A professor is someone
who talks in someone
else's sleep.*

W. H. AUDEN

Bringing out the
Best in Me.

I guess if I weren't an actor, I'd be a history professor.

TOM BERENGER

Our progress as a nation can be no swifter than our progress in education. The human mind is our fundamental resource.

JOHN F. KENNEDY

A teacher can be a 'guru', a 'maestro', a 'mentor', a 'tutor', an 'instructor', a 'coach'... or a superstar.

The very spring and root
of honesty and virtue lie
in good education.

PLUTARCH

I am indebted to my father for living, but to my teacher for living well.

ALEXANDER THE GREAT

Great teachers...

keep your teeth clean

. . . teach life, not just their lessons.

Good teachers make the best of a pupil's means; great teachers foresee a pupil's ends.

MARIA CALLAS

One looks back with appreciation to the brilliant teachers, but with gratitude to those who touched our human feelings.

CARL JUNG

You deserve an award for:

Being the Kindest, Most Special Teacher.

*A teacher is one
who makes himself
progressively unnecessary.*

THOMAS CARRUTHERS

Great teachers...

... are always proud to see their students succeed.

If you're interested in finding out more about our gift books follow us on Twitter: **@Summersdale**

www.summersdale.com